TRUE TALES OF RESCUE

TIGER TIME

KAMA EINHORN

HOUGHTON MIFFLIN HARCOURT
Boston New York

hmhbooks.com

The text type was set in Jolly Good Sans.
Book design by Tom Carling.

Library of Congress Cataloging-in-Publication Data
Names: Einhorn, Kama, 1969- author.
Title: Tiger time / Kama Einhorn.
Description: Boston : Houghton Mifflin Harcourt, [2019] | Series: True tales
of rescue | Audience: Age 7-10. | Audience: Grade 4 to 6.
Identifiers: LCCN 2019000889 (print) | LCCN 2019002432 (ebook) | ISBN
9780358164340 (ebook) | ISBN 9781328767073 (paper over board) | ISBN
Subjects: LCSH: Tiger--Juvenile literature. | Wildlife rescue--Juvenile
literature. | Animal sanctuaries--Colorado--Juvenile literature.
Classification: LCC QL737.C23 (ebook) | LCC QL737.C23 E38 2019 (print) | DDC
599.756--dc23
LC record available at https://lccn.loc.gov/2019000889

Manufactured in Malaysia
TWP 10 9 8 7 6 5 4 3 2 1
4500769320

Author's note: This book is inspired by the true stories of the Wild Animal Sanctuary in Colorado, and it is full of real facts about tigers and sanctuary life. But it's also "creative" nonfiction—because tigers don't talk, at least not in ways that humans can understand! Some of the tigers described are actually composites of several different animals, and certain details—including locations, events, and timing—have been changed. Also, some human dialogue has been reconstructed from memory.

This book is not a manual on how to rescue wildlife, nor is it meant to provide any actual directions on caring for tigers or any other animal. Every situation is different. If you see any creature in trouble, contact a licensed wildlife rehabilitator right away.

*For Pat Craig and Kent Drotar,
the staff and volunteers of the
Wild Animal Sanctuary,
the 3,900 tigers left in the wild,
and the 15,000 tigers still living in cages
in the United States.*

CONTENTS

4

HOPE & HAVEN:
ANIMAL SANCTUARIES

A sanctuary is a place where living beings are kept safe from harm and are free to be themselves.

Humans have created animal sanctuaries—protected places for injured, orphaned, or threatened animals. In many sanctuaries, people prepare animals for their return to the wild. If that's not an option, the animals spend the rest of their lives protected, in as natural a habitat as possible.

At sanctuaries, humans lend a helping hand.

Animal sanctuaries exist for different reasons. Like most sanctuary animals, the five hundred animals at the Wild Animal Sanctuary (WAS) in Colorado are there because of problems humans have created. There

The Wild Animal Sanctuary is in the High Plains of Colorado. You can see the Rocky Mountains.

WYOMING

NEBRASKA

•Keenesburg
•Denver

COLORADO

•Colorado Springs

KANSAS

NEW MEXICO

are only about 3,900 tigers left in the wild, but there are about fifteen thousand tigers living in cages in the United States—in zoos, in circuses, and in homes, as pets. It's not a good way for any animal to live, but some get rescued and brought to WAS, the oldest sanctuary of its kind in the world.

Since 1980, WAS has rescued and cared for lions, tigers, bears, leopards, jaguars, mountain lions, and some smaller carnivores such as wolves, servals, bobcats, lynx, foxes, coyotes, and coatimundi. There have also been alpacas and horses, a few emus, several ostriches, one porcupine, one raccoon, and one camel. (You'll also see hundreds of prairie dogs poking their heads up from their burrows, but they haven't been rescued—they just live there!)

The people who run sanctuaries are serious about their work, but they wish they didn't have to do it in the first place. They wish there were no need for animal sanctuaries and that the world was safer for animals. They teach people about the animals' situations and encourage them to help.

There can be plenty of heartbreak in any sanctuary's story, but there are also lots of happy endings. The more you know about why sanctuaries are important and what people can do to help, the better off all animals everywhere will be.

SANCTUARY STEPS

Each sanctuary is different, but they all do some or all of the following things, in the order below. WAS handles all four phases:

- **Rescue:** Humans step in, remove animals from harm, and bring them to safety. Rescue situations are usually emergencies.

- **Recovery:** Licensed wildlife caregivers treat the animals for injuries or illnesses, create a recovery plan, and let them rest and heal.

- **Rehabilitation:** The caregivers encourage the animals' natural instincts. Some "wild" behaviors have to be taught, while some animals simply know what to do. Sometimes the animals must learn by watching one another.

- **Release:** Caregivers help animals live in their natural habitats (or as similiar to that as possible) the way they were meant to.

WELL, IT'S ABOUT TIME!

Wow. It's 3:30 in the morning and thirty-nine of you have just arrived at the Wild Animal Sanctuary (WAS). Now there are eighty-eight of us living here . . . on 789 acres of rolling grasslands.

Welcome, new tigers. I'm Kamal. I'm a mellow fellow.

We've never had such a large group of tigers come here at one time. I could hear your huge trailer trucks bumping and clanging through the half-frozen dirt roads of our habitat, your cages loaded carefully inside. You had been traveling for twelve hours straight, with your rescuers taking turns at the wheel, and giving you food and water along the way.

I bet it got warm in those trailers, but soon you'll experience December on the High Plains of Colorado, and out here, it's

My name Kamal means "perfection," "beauty," and "excellence" in Arabic. In Hindi, it means "pale red."

absolutely freezing. When the sun comes up you'll see the Rocky Mountains in the distance. Their snow-capped tops are pointy, and in certain light the rock looks a little purple. Since all of us tigers descend from frigid, rocky Siberia, Colorado is a very nice place to be.

You couldn't tell from your cages at the back of the trailer, but the humans driving these trucks are so tired that their whole bodies ache. At their feet were a dozen empty Styrofoam coffee cups. They'd bought drinks quickly at truck stops, because they drove straight through to get you here as fast as they could. They didn't want you to be in your rescue cages any longer than you had to be—you'd been in cages for long enough!

Your trailers were banging along on roads

that go right along the fence of my habitat, so I could walk along the edge and follow you as you moved by. Some staff vehicles, like the food and supply trucks, go along this road all day, so my two habitat-mates, Simon and Sophie, and I are called "the driveway tigers."

The animals all know when the forty-foot (12-meter) rescue trailer trucks arrive. Every time. The humans are always surprised and amused by our reactions. We're like a welcoming committee—we rush to the fences at the edge of our habitats and celebrate in our own ways. We tigers come to the fence and put our front paws up and stare. The lions roar and bellow; the ground vibrates. Wolves howl *ah-ooo:* their welcome song. The lynx pace and meow loudly, and the foxes jump around silently. If the bears aren't hibernating (which they are right now), they stand up on their hind legs. Leopards flick their tails and stand up like us, paws on fences.

And the humans high-five and hug. They congratulate one another because they've pulled off quite a feat, getting you to safety. First they'll get you settled and comfortable, keeping you in new cages where you can move around and calm down; then they'll go take well-deserved naps as a fresh team takes over.

RESCUE

Time for a Change

CHAPTER 1

THiS TiGER'S TaLe

You came from a terrible and terrifying place, I know. Otherwise you wouldn't be here. After each rescue, the humans often have nightmares about the places from which they freed more animals. But very soon—perhaps right away, but probably within a few weeks—you'll see that this place is the opposite of where you've been, and hopefully you'll forget the worst of your old life.

I've forgotten most of my early days, but I remember that I'd been living in a dog crate with a man in his car. The man didn't have a permanent home. My buddy, Diesel, also lived in a crate in that car. The man must have really needed money, because he let tourists pay to take pictures with us and cuddle us. We hated it. We were also getting bigger and more dangerous, so he'd give us drugs to keep us sleepy and relatively harmless. It was too bad he didn't have a real home and maybe a little housecat, because he sure wasn't thinking of what was best for wild animals.

Someone finally told the police about us. The police called the local Society for the Prevention of Cruelty to Animals (SPCA), who had heard about Pat Craig and his sanctuary.

The SPCA called the sanctuary to see if they could take us, and Pat said yes. He and his teenage son, Casey, drove eighteen hours in

MY FRIEND PAT CRAIg

Almost forty years ago, nineteen-year-old Pat Craig visited a friend working at a zoo in North Carolina. His friend showed him tigers and lions in small cages hidden from the visitors. The zoo had only a few cages for tigers, and the zoo owners wanted to show visitors only the cute babies. They had no room for the tigers that had grown too big or old, so those animals either stayed in those cages or were euthanized ("put to sleep").

their little truck to come pick us up. Diesel and I were loaded into Pat's truck in our carriers, and our life in the man's car faded away.

Back at his family farmhouse near Boulder, Colorado, Pat had to do something. He used his grandmother's typewriter to tap out seventy-five letters to zoos across the country, asking if they had extra animals needing a new home. At the same time, he got all the right government permits and licenses he needed to build some decent habitats on his family farm.

Finally, a zoo in South Carolina said they had a baby jaguar that could use a home. Pat flew there and brought little Freckles back on the airplane. He had never even seen a real baby jaguar. Neither had the flight attendants, because they believed him when he said she was just a Himalayan—an exotic breed of housecat!

Pat carried us right into the sanctuary's clinic so the vet could examine us. Diesel and I both had ringworm (a skin fungus, not a worm). We hadn't been fed well; we were malnourished. Pat gave us cut-up chicken breast and held bottles of formula in our mouths. We were still playful cubs, and we

Pat's work is known all over the world now. He's even a professor, teaching about the captive-animal crisis. Pat lives with his wife and kids in a home right over the clinic.

Mondo gives his friend Pat a smooch.

stayed with Pat at his house as we needed so many bottles each day! His place also had a big outdoor playpen, and he had a pack of playful, gentle dogs (he still does). They helped raise us, in a way. That dog pack has raised quite a few of the wild animals here.

💛 Kamal's Baby Book 💛

My friends Timmy
and Simon.

We loved to lick Pat's arms and head with our huge, rough tongues, but soon the day came when we licked his hair right off! After all, our tongues are made for cleaning meat off bone. No more playtime with Pat for us! We moved to a large cage outside the house, and soon Pat started taking us to visit Big Athos, a huge adult tiger. He became like another dad to us, and eventually, we moved into his habitat.

Diesel had many happy, healthy years here until he got sick and died a few years ago. Now I consider it my job to enjoy life enough for the both of us. I think he'd be happy to know that.

Pat visits a lot. My habitat has tall prairie grass and a pond, and it's the size of a football field! I can see Pat coming from really far away. I can even tell if he's looking right at me, because I can see the white part of his eyeballs! I always rush right over to the chainlink fence. I lie down and let him scratch me through the holes, rubbing my whiskers against the metal wires. I love the smell of my old friend. But Pat knows he can't come in to play with me anymore—I'm so big and strong that if I play too rough, I could really hurt him. I live like a real tiger now. If humans have to come into our habitats for any reason, they stay in enclosed vehicles. You may be wondering if they have to come in and clean out our poop. They don't, because our habitats are big enough that they can just let the poop biodegrade—break down naturally and become part of the soil.

Well, that's my story. Every animal here has a different one. Soon I'll learn yours.

GOOD BUDDIES

Me and Simon and Sophie—triple trouble!

Unlike lions, who are all about their prides (groups), tigers are pretty independent. But we'll often have a few friends, especially here at the sanctuary, where we don't have to compete for food.

I've always been very protective of my habitat-mates, Simon and Sophie. I'm the oldest. They were born here because their mom was pregnant with them when she was rescued.

Simon's my best friend. We romp and play plenty. He's bigger and heavier than me, but he still acts like a cub.

CHAPTER 2

39 SAD STORIES

Well. Now that the sun's up and I've heard some humans talking as they unloaded more of your supplies near me, I've learned more about you.

First of all, none of you are cubs, like I was when I got here. You've been living in cages— barely big enough for you to turn around in— for a long time. Years and years.

You came from Oklahoma, owned by a company that called itself a "rescue group." But your owners were actually selling tickets to people so they could swim in a pool with you when you were cubs. I know this must have been miserable. You were separated from your moms and being crowded by strange humans in the water. Once you got bigger, you weren't of much use to your owners any longer, and you were stored away in a dark room. Many of you females were forced to have more cubs.

Most humans describe tigers as majestic, regal, and elegant. But they wouldn't have used those words if they'd seen you there—they'd have said you were depressed and pitiful.

"Swimming with tiger cubs," one staff member sighed loudly this morning. "You think you've seen it all, but then there's some new horrible idea."

The owner finally agreed to let you go, because he was having money problems. The team here was ready to rescue as many of you as they legally could, and they sprang into action.

TiGER RESCUE iN 10 EASY STEPS: INSTRUCTiONS FOR HUMANS

 Do the math. How many tigers will you be picking up? You'll need one specially designed rescue cage per tiger, and you can fit eight cages per truck. (Pat's son, Casey, and another staffer, Ryan Clements, design and weld the cages here.)

 Wheel the empty cages into the trucks along with lots of medical equipment. Remember your walkie-talkies—you'll have to communicate from different locations, working together (or there will be problems . . . guaranteed!).

Drive the trucks to the rescue site (the longest trip WAS ever made was twenty-two hours from Colorado to Miami, where animals had been flown into the port from Argentina!). You'll need two people per truck so you can take turns driving. At least one vet needs to join your whole group.

On the way, figure out how you'll actually get to the animals. You may have to call the police to protect you; you might need lawyers to remind people of the laws; or you may need special equipment to cut through fences. Each situation's different.

 Once you're there, put on your fluorescent orange shirts so everyone can tell from far away that you're on the team. Look at the animals to figure out who might not move calmly into the rescue cages. Those animals will need to be tranquilized with a dart gun, moved onto a stretcher (by four strong humans), and slid into a rescue cage.

 For the other tigers, open the gate of each rescue cage and push it up against the cages the tigers are in, so that the two cages are attached. Drop pieces of raw meat into the rescue cages, then pull up the gate. When the tigers go toward the meat, they feel like they're walking from one "room" into another.

 Close the gates of the rescue cages and pull them away from the old cages. Wheel the rescue cages back into the trucks using the ramp. They'll be much heavier this time! Right away, give each animal water, vitamins, and antibiotics (because they're all very likely to have some kind of infection).

That's Pat on the right.

8 Turn around and drive straight back. Take turns at the wheel and drink a lot of coffee on the way. Listen to loud music to stay awake; talk about how the rescue went; and plan what you're going to do when you get back.

9 Stop only to fill up your gas tank. Park in a spot that's as private as possible so you can open the back and check on the tigers quickly. Don't mention to anyone there that you have eight tigers in your truck.

10 When you arrive at WAS, help get the animals settled. Let some new humans take over so you can pass out. Tomorrow is another day!

It's been a long road. Ready to come out of that tiny cage?

The staff had only a few early-morning hours to get you all out, because the owners of the place wanted to let customers in at nine, as they always do. They didn't want to lose any business.

As always, everyone on the WAS team had a specific role, and some people from Oklahoma animal rescue groups came to help out. Like other tigers during their rescues, you looked closely at the humans, paying attention to figure out who was in charge. Which human was the leader? You had to "read" the situation. We do this to be "ahead of the game"—we have to know who's our best bet for survival, who will help us—that's the dominant human (in case you haven't figured it out, that would be Pat). It's just like dogs know who's really in charge of their human family. We

may be cats, but in this way, we're a bit like dogs. (Pat says we're like dogs in tiger suits!)

It was quite an operation. You all seemed to relax and enjoy the movement on the eight-

Loading and unloading any big animal's rescue cage is hard work.

hour drive. Those of you who are siblings or buddies were placed right next to one another.

Until they start driving back, the humans have been "on a high." The whole mission so far has been *go! go! go!* as fast as they can, without a minute to relax. It's not until they start driving away with you safe and sound behind them that their minds start to unwind a little. They start going over how it went, who among you was limping, who had sores, and what care you may need once you get here.

I'm sure you were very happy to know that the first stop upon arrival was the Carnivore Nutrition Center . . . to pick up lots of raw meat!

WHO'S WHO

As soon as the humans arrived to rescue you, Becca, the head of the medical care team here, tried to start taking notes on each of you for your records. She asked the owners your names, but they didn't really have an answer. You had names, but the owners just called you "that tiger" or "this tiger here" or "that cat over there." To them, you weren't unique individuals. But believe me . . . now you are! The team had to give most of you new names, and it doesn't take them long to remember who's who.

You'll soon learn to recognize your names. The humans will learn your different personalities and quirks, and especially your favorite kind of meat (for instance, I prefer beef over poultry). They learn the things that thrill you and the things that annoy you. They'll be totally devoted to making you as happy as possible. It may take an hour or it may take a few years, but don't worry. They're on it.

A group of tigers is called a streak or an ambush! And here you all are . . . the biggest streak the sanctuary has ever rescued at once. .

Almadala

Bailee

Bella

Bo

Brutus

Clarence

Clay

Curly

Daniel

Enzo

Hope

Katniss

King Edwards

King Mosiah

Larry

Lilly

Mecan

Meeka

Meg

Missouri

Mobo

Moe

Moose

Nakita

Noelle

Pearl

Peeta

Rambo

Rocky

Roy

Tajah

Tarzan

Thomas

Thunder

Toni

Tora

Vader

Wakeen

Zeke

And here are the tigers who live here already:

- **Athos, Simon**, and **Sophie** were born here (their moms were rescued tigers).

- **Angel, Anna, Bazooka, Cricket, Leche, Reggie, Gary, Natalya**, and **Tyrone** are from California.

- **Shela, T. J.**, and **Tahoe** are from Minnesota.

- **Jevie** is from Nebraska.

- **Chase** is from Missouri.

- **Jimmy** is from Kansas.

- **Sierra** is from Illinois.

- **Silly, Toby, Mary Jane**, and **Hamilton** are from Texas.

- **Mowgli, Kiara**, and **Simba** are from Idaho.

- **Milo** and **Timara** are from Ohio.

- **Yoya, Cucho, Diego, Frieda I**, and **Frieda II** are from Mexico.

- **Songa** is from Georgia.

- **Grumpy** and **Raphael** are from South Dakota.

Most of the states above have no laws against owning exotic pets. And if they do have laws, they are often not enforced. Sigh.

CHAPTER 3
SAFE CAGES

By now you've entered your safe cages, which are plopped right in the middle of a much bigger space. That larger space is what will eventually become your real, open habitats. The people started building rows and rows of these habitats with safe cages inside them months before they were even sure they'd be able to rescue you, because they'd heard about you and knew there was a good chance they'd be able to bring you here. They built fifty cages and started preparing forty acres of habitats (that's about forty football fields). Better to have too many than not enough!

While you're busy recovering, Ryan and Casey will be working eighteen-hour days to finish building your habitats.

Soon you'll take your first step into your new life, Brutus—
you don't even know how good it'll be!

Can you smell
the safety of
the safe cage,
Roy?

Go ahead,
Katniss....
You're almost
there.

You're in! Lots to check out.

The local power company donates tall, strong wooden telephone poles. Ryan and Casey cut them to the right size, plant them in concrete, and put up wire fencing. Your whole area will look like a construction site for a little while, but you'll get used to it.

Look at all this open space.

The safe cages are much bigger than the ones you were in before, of course. First of all, they're outside in the cleanest, freshest air you've every sniffed. There's enough room to move, play, eat, drink, and sleep. But the safe cages aren't huge. You wouldn't know what to do with too much space—yet.

You have everything you need in your safe cages. Your water containers are refilled every day (they're chained to the fence so the humans can easily refill them with a hose from outside and so you can't throw them around and play with them . . . sorry!). The clean floors are made of concrete, and each cage has a good log to stretch out on or use to scratch yourself. You also have your own den in there—a concrete box with a hole for an entrance. Like all dens, it keeps you cool in summer and warm in winter.

The humans will feed you often. They'll put fresh meat through the bars with tongs. Some of you will grab the meat right from the tongs; others will wait for the humans to drop the meat and then eat only once the coast is clear. Only a few humans will be allowed to visit you so you'll get used to them slowly and begin to trust them. They won't bug you, but they're paying close attention to how you're doing. Sometimes they'll bring you surprise treats, like drumsticks. Ryan and Casey will be building your play structures, too. Just you wait! (Ryan has always worked as a builder, but he also wanted to help animals—now he gets to do both. He used to volunteer here on weekends. He lived a few hours away, so he would drive here and sleep in his car at a gas station, so he could work both weekend days.)

You'll stay in your safe cages as long as you like. Most tigers stay for a few weeks. Eventually, the humans open the gate and you are free to step into your larger habitat. You decide when to step out; they'll encourage you by putting your food just outside the cage. You can go back and forth as you please. By then, most of you will know you're safe.

Ready for some real food?

CHAPTER 4

PANTHERA TIGRIS

I hear you're settling in well, but you still barely know what it means to live like a real tiger (scientific name: *Panthera tigris*).

Now that you're beginning to stretch, play, stalk, roll, jump, swim, and hide, I thought you might enjoy learning all about your amazing big-cat bodies.

Depending on our subspecies—what kind of tiger we are—we can grow as long as eleven feet (3.3 meters) and weigh up to 670 pounds (303 kilograms).

Our fur is as soft as a housecat's! (Most humans think it would be rough or wiry, but then most humans haven't petted us!) Our fur can be pumpkin-colored, copper, dark orange, biscuit-orange, light orange, or white. Our bellies, chests, and throats are always white or creamy white. Our faces have white markings.

Our paws are humongous furry paddles—thunderpaws! Our paw pads let us climb, grasp, and silently stalk prey. We use our "thumbs" to hold meat down as we pull it apart with our teeth.

We keep our claws sharp by scratching trees or logs. The first claw on each front foot never touches the ground!

Our vertical stripes camouflage us in tall grasses. We each have a unique pattern. If we were shaved, you'd see that our skin itself is striped!

Our thick tails help us balance as we turn quickly. We also use them to communicate: a loose, hanging tail means we're relaxed; flicking it from side to side or holding it low and twitchy means we're feeling aggressive.

Our legs and shoulders practically explode with muscle power! Our bones are thick and our frames are sturdy. Our hind legs are longer than our front legs, making us amazing jumpers.

Our heads weigh about sixty pounds (27 kilograms.) That's about as much as a whole seven-year-old kid. Look closely at Hannibal's pretty face!

Our ears are rounded, not pointy like a housecat's. In the wild, we use our sharp sense of hearing for hunting—we hear sounds humans can't.

Our whiskers are the main way we use our sense of touch. We each have five types of whiskers with sensitive nerves—without them, we'd be confused as to how to move through our habitats.

Our teeth... obviously a big deal. Our long canines (fangs) are up to three inches (7.6 centimeters) long! We have lots of nerves in our gums that make us expert biters.

Our eyes are the color of gold. We see six times better than humans at night. White tigers have blue eyes! Our eyes work like binoculars, and if we see humans we don't know, we'll freeze.

Our noses are very important. We communicate with each other by marking our territories (spraying our strong-smelling pee!). Mammals' hair follicles hold each individual's smell—if you brought me just one short hair off Pat's head, I'd know it was his!

Our tongues are rough because they're covered in thousands of papillae, or sharp barbs, so that we can rasp (lick meat off bones).

53

THE FELINE FAMILY

We are all part of the feline family tree.

LIONS

COUGAR   CHEETAH

LYNX

BLACK JAGUAR

SERVAL

SNOW LEOPARD

HOUSECAT

TiGER TYPES

There are six existing subspecies of tigers. Most of us here are mixes. Over the last one hundred years, 95 percent of us have disappeared. Of all the big cats, we're the closest to extinction.

Bengal tigers live in the tropical rainforests, marshes, and tall grasses of India.

Siberian/Amur are the biggest tigers!

South China tigers may be extinct already.

Indochinese tigers are disappearing faster than any other tiger.

There are fewer than 250 **Malayan** tigers in the world.

Sumatran tigers are the smallest.

PART 2

RECOVERY

Taking a Time-Out

CHAPTER 5

THE ROUND HOUSE

For most arriving tigers, recovery starts in a very special shelter called the Round House. I live right next door. (You didn't go there because there are too many of you, and I didn't go because I was too little.) It's the oldest part of the sanctuary.

From above, the Round House looks like a pizza cut into sixteen slices—each tiger gets a slice. The wider parts of the slices are outdoors, and the tips of the slices are indoor dens. Inside each slice, there's a big, round aboveground pool to play in, a bin of water to drink from, some toys, and a log to scratch, stretch on, and lie on.

The wider part of the slices are outdoors, and the tips of the slices are indoor dens.

Only a few humans take care of the Round House tigers. The Round House is a good place for them to get to know us. We arrive in different states: depressed, calm, starving, fearful of humans, agitated, friendly, playful, or shy. The humans start a file for each of us and write notes in it every day, including detailed medical plans. They also start figuring out which tigers might do well sharing a habitat.

Usually each tiger gets his or her own slice of the Round House, because many have never even seen another tiger. It's designed so that they can look right through their fences though, into the next slice, to get used to other tigers.

As the Round House tigers sleep in their dens, the caregivers close the den gates so they can clean the cages and change the water. They also move the logs every time, since we need variety.

Most of the Round House tigers arrive malnourished, which causes lots of different medical problems. We big cats are carnivores; we only eat meat. We have to—our bodies need protein and can't get it from any other food.

Nala and Simba, safe in their pizza slice!

But even in the Round House, we get fed just a few times a week. Our bodies are designed to digest food that way. One big feeding keeps us full a long time, and we always get more meat than we need. That's good for the animals who come here starving, because eventually it sinks in that there's always enough. So now please allow me to explain our menu, because you'll find it quite scrumptious.

Lunchtime.

UP IN THE AIR

All around the Round House and the whole sanctuary, thousands of birds constantly flutter, twitter, squawk, and chirp high above (and down low). Most of them eat our leftovers; no meat here ever goes to waste. They all swoop down for scraps . . . once we've walked away from our meals, that is (they're no dummies)!

The starlings are the "junk birds"—they love our food, and it sounds like there are a million of them. Seagulls, too. In January and February, we see birds of prey: American eagles, bald eagles, prairie falcons, kestrels, red-tailed hawks, and golden eagles. They're all such good hunters . . . they're like the tigers of the bird world. There are lots of other native birds here: great blue herons, Canada geese, red-winged blackbirds, house sparrows, swallows, doves, magpies, wild turkeys, and more.

CHAPTER 6

TIGER PIE

Much of recovery is about eating well. We don't get fed at set times like housecats or animals in zoos, because in the wild our meals would be random! We can eat up to thirty pounds (14 kilograms) of meat at once. It takes us about three short minutes to eat an entire raw chicken thrown over our fences.

Because we always get enough meat, we don't get anxious and fight over food. In the wild, we only fight about three things—food, territory, and mates. The humans here take care of these problems before they begin. They give us plenty of safe territory, and we don't have to compete for mates because we're either kept separate or neutered, if male (to keep us from making babies). It's a peaceful existence.

It's actually not that easy to buddy us up, because we're so independent. But if we can avoid those three problems, we do fine. We can be social enough to have a buddy or two, and we'll give each other friendly head bumps and chin rubs.

The whole feeding process begins at the Carnivore Nutrition Center. It's pretty much the center of this place. The staff unloads all our meat as it arrives in big trucks— fifty-eight large department stores in the Denver area donate sixty thousand pounds (more than 27,000 kilograms) of food every week. That's the weight of fifty cars, enough raw meat to make 240,000 hamburgers. After all, just one tiger can eat a hundred pounds (45 kilograms) of raw meat per week.

Step one of Tiger Pie!

The trucks pull up and the staff and volunteers unload the trucks, sort the meat, and prepare it according to the needs of each species. (Even though the meat is donated, it still costs $400,000 a year to keep us fed because WAS pays for the trucks, gas, electricity for the refrigerators, and staff!)

In my opinion, the best thing about the Carnivore Nutrition Center is this: It's where Tiger Pie is made.

TiGER PIE
By the Carnivore Kitchen's prep cooks and chefs

One ten-pound (4.5-kilogram) pie feeds one tiger, so make a batch of eighty-eight at a time!

1. Pull beef, pork, chicken, turkey, and duck from the big buckets.

2. Grind it together in the huge grinding machine.

3. Add eggs, vitamins, minerals, supplements, like algae and calcium powder for healthy bones.

4. Press the mixture into round pans (ten pounds per pan), stack them in the freezer, and then, once frozen, pop them out of the pan. Presto—Tiger Pie!

5. Load the pies onto the food carts. Caregivers will drive around to the habitats and hurl the pies over the tigers' fences.

We all love our pies, and each of us eats them differently. Some of us gnaw on them frozen, some lick them as they slowly thaw so that the meal takes a while to eat, and some wait for them to thaw completely and then gobble them up all at once!

Honey's lunch.

Feeding the bears at WAS is a different story. They get a combination of fruits, vegetables, seafood, and raw and cooked meat. Bears have ridiculous sweet tooths. They'll fight over grapes and melons. For the coyotes, coatis, and the porcupine, it's all about the cheese!

Our bodies are built to hunt, gorge, and recover. Our stomachs can hold a lot; we can even go two weeks without food. But when we do get fed, it's a party.

CHAPTER 7

WHAT COULD HAVE BEEN

While I'm talking about meat, it's time for me to tell you the truth about what could have been, if we'd been born in the wild and stayed there. We'd have been expert hunters. It wouldn't necessarily have been an easy life, but it would have been a wild one. As predators, we'd have been fierce and aggressive. We'll never experience that.

Although the meat here is delicious and plentiful, someone other than us brought us these animals. We only get to eat someone else's kill. This is kind of a bummer; we don't know what we're missing, but you must admit it sounds pretty enchanting:

We'd have hunted alone, expertly stalking our prey by moonlight, or maybe by the dim light of dawn or dusk. A lot of hunting involves moving slowly and sitting still, but when it was time to pounce, we'd have been fast. We're big and heavy, but we can run as fast as a car on a highway. We'd have known the exact moment to pounce on a deer, wild pig, water buffalo, bison, moose, bear, or tapir. If there was nothing else to hunt, we'd have eaten rabbits, leopards, pythons, crocodiles, wild dogs, monkeys, porcupines, fish, or even birds.

We'd have hidden nearby in the tall grass, camouflaging ourselves to stalk an animal. We wouldn't have made a sound. Our prey usually don't even see us coming. We'd have crept toward them slowly and jumped, surprising them so they'd have had little chance to escape. We'd have leapt more

Even though I don't hunt, I'm still an expert stalker, leaper, and pouncer. I'm so fast, I look like a blur!

than thirty feet (9 meters) in one jump! We'd have come at them from the side or from behind, and killed them fast by clawing or biting the neck (or the back of the head), so they would have died right away.

Then we'd have dragged our prey to a nearby safe place to feast on it (even dragging it through water if we had to). We may have covered our leftovers in dirt so we could snack later. Once in a while, we'd have shared our meat with other tigers. We'd have found fresh cool water from streams and lakes and lapped up as much as we needed.

Most humans see us hunting only on nature shows. They often find it upsetting, but that's the way it is—there's a food chain, and we'd have been the apex predators. That means we'd have been "top of the food chain," or superpredators—no other animal would have eaten us.

But tigers just don't have enough habitat to live in anymore. Only a hundred years ago, about a hundred thousand of us wild tigers roamed across most of Asia. Now, only about four thousand tigers are out there in those savannas, snowy mountains, tropical forests, evergreen forests, woodlands, mangrove swamps, and grasslands.

We live in just 4 percent of our old habitat because humans have built roads, homes, or factories, or they use our habitat to grow their own crops. Humans also poach us—they can sell our pelts (our fur coats) or use our body parts to make medicine that people believe will make them more powerful. Sometimes humans hunt us just for fun, just to say they killed a tiger! Then they display our heads on their walls, like trophies. Big sigh.

Many humans all over the world are trying to solve these problems. For now, the staff and volunteers here keep making us Tiger Pie.

CHAPTER 8

TiGER TREATMENT

Recovery isn't just about eating meat; it's also about veterinary care. Our vets specialize in big animals. There's a university near here with big-cat experts, and they come to the clinic at least once a week to take care of us. Big cats usually arrive with two big problems.

One is our enormous paws. Most of us were declawed before we got to this sanctuary. It makes us less dangerous to humans, but it really messes us up—it's like a human losing the first section of a finger. After all, we're meant to use our claws to hunt and defend ourselves, and even if we don't need to do those things here, not having claws feels deeply wrong to us. Plus being declawed hurts (and if the operation hasn't been done properly, our paws keep hurting, so some of us stay on pain medication our whole lives.) Being declawed also damages our balance, so it can hurt our leg bones.

The other problem is our teeth. Obviously, we are born with teeth that become giant, impressive fangs. But humans have either filed them down (for the same reasons they declaw us), or we've been so stressed out in our cages that we've used them to bite and pull at the bars.

Because our teeth are infected and painful, we need root canal therapy (most adult humans cringe at these words!). We can also get gum disease from bad nutrition and no vet care. We can't eat meat without them.

Even if they fed us pureed meat like you'd feed to a housecat, it's psychologically bad for us to have no teeth (just like it is to have no claws). And physically, our teeth are more important to us than humans' are to them. When we lose our teeth, our jawbones get weak, so our skulls do too.

When Fireball arrived, he was miserable and growled constantly. After his root canals, he was a totally different tiger!

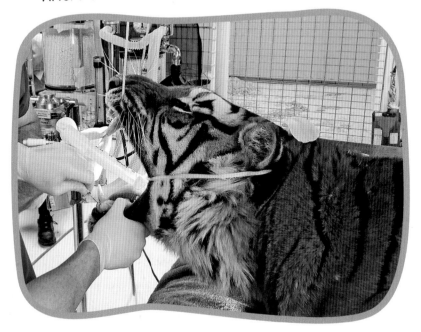

Getting us onto a surgery table can be a challenge. First they have to tranquilize us in our habitat; then a team transports us to the clinic and hoists us up onto the table with a special pulley. We're totally unconscious during the surgery. Usually we need root canals on at least three of our four fangs; each takes an hour. If we're male, we get neutered at the same time (to keep us from getting female tigers pregnant).

The humans also remove a few pieces of our fur to send to university researchers, because our hair follicles hold hormones that tell how stressed we are. The researchers want to know if our hormone levels change from the time we were rescued from our tiny cages to the time when we're in our nice big habitats. If the researchers can prove that we're less stressed after we're rescued, it will be a good argument to convince people to give us more space.

When we wake up, we're in a clinic cage by ourselves, and the people watch us closely to make sure we're okay. They also begin to majorly spoil us. They might put on music or play movies—we seem to like that as we wake up. They may also put lavender oil near our noses to keep us calm.

I haven't been to the clinic since I was a cub, since we can be treated for most problems right in our habitats. They'll just stick medicine right into our meat.

Our medical problems can make us plain old cranky. We can't begin to be rehabilitated when we're cranky, and rehabbing is the whole point. So let me explain what rehab means.

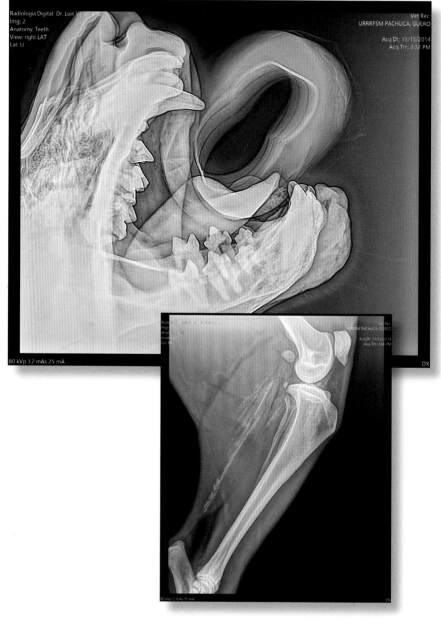

INSIDE A TIGER

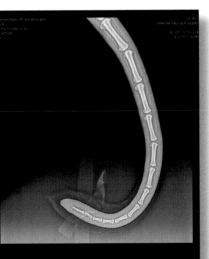

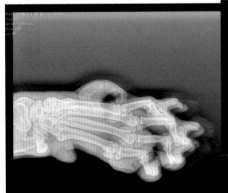

Once we're released from the clinic, a cool dip in our new habitat feels magical.

PART 3

REHABILITATION

Take Your Time!

CHAPTER 9

HABITATS FOR HAPPINESS

Recovery is about getting physically well, but rehab is about our emotional health—just learning how to live as happy, normal tigers, as close as possible to how we would live in the wild. It means learning to explore our habitats, feel confident, enjoy our dens, play in water, make a friend or two, lie in the sun, hide in tall grasses and build our trust. (Many of you will growl and crouch when humans come near. That makes sense right now.)

Pat says that the humans here have to understand where we came from; it's a big piece of figuring out the rehab puzzle. When he goes on rescues, Pat looks carefully

Big cats with aches and pains, like Lightning, get special beds.

at where we've been living, and what our experience has been. Were we kept in the dark? What size was our cage? Did we see other tigers or have tiger friends? What's it going to take to get each of us healthy?

Another staff member, Kent, explains it like

this: "Their life has been one deep hole. When they come here, they're still in that hole. So first you gotta fill up the hole, get them to level ground. Only then can you rehab them."

Living in that "hole" is why lots of us are neurotic when we arrive—we might be anxious, depressed, act obsessively, and have other symptoms of stress and distress. For instance, if we've never gotten enough food, we might become very possessive of it, and get aggressive if we think anyone is coming to take it from us.

Lots of lions come here without ever having roared. Can you believe that? For them, filling up the hole means putting them with other lions so they learn how to communicate and become part of a pride. When they roar to one another, Kent and the staff know their holes are filling up.

Chase is a tiger who has been in his hole for a while now. He's had a hard time since he got here a few years ago, and he's still not crazy about people. He was paired with another tiger at first, but he growled at him. He bites himself. The humans here will keep trying to help. He's only six, so he has lots of time to learn; he's actually been getting a little better lately. His body seems more relaxed when he lies in the sun, and he's biting himself less.

Bears have other problems. One bear, Trouble, was trained to perform in a circus. Like dogs, he got treats for doing tricks. When he arrived and the humans approached with treats, he'd start doing his whole performance routine—standing on his head, balancing a ball on his nose—not knowing he didn't need to do that anymore. He didn't understand that the humans were giving him treats just to make him

Some bears must learn to hibernate.

happy. But slowly, over time, Trouble stopped doing his tricks.

And Tanaka the bear had been kept in a woman's backyard with no place to hibernate . . . so he didn't know how! The first winter he was here, when most of the other bears were snoozing underground, he just wouldn't go into his den and lie down, even though the humans filled his warm concrete room with wood chips and straw. It takes some bears a few winters to catch on, but eventually they all do.

One bear refused to leave the original rescue cage once it was unloaded from the truck he arrived in. He wouldn't move into his safe cage. The humans put food in there, but he'd just reach far out to get it and drag it right back into his little rescue cage. The staff just watched and sighed sadly. "They know what we want them to do," Pat reminded his team. "But they're gonna do it in their own time. Rushing them never helps."

Abby's morning soak.

Leon and Leo enjoying sanctuary life.

We each get a rehab plan. The humans carefully choose our habitat-mates—one or two tigers we'll get along with. Sometimes they let us live alone. Because no matter what, a huge part of rehab is our habitats—they're our entire world. And most of us have never lived in the world of a tiger, so our habitats are where we learn.

All the tiger habitats here are similar. They're huge—at least the size of one football field, and usually bigger. There are fences between each; eastern red cedar trees, cottonwood trees, lilac bushes, and sand cherry bushes run along them for privacy and shade. We're under the big Colorado sky, and our air is crisp and fresh. There's tall, lush grass to hide in and a pond or pool, plus toys, play structures, and logs. And we each get our own den, just like we'd have in the wild.

Mili and Brownie, the lazy coyotes.

The hard earth floor is covered in a layer of wood chips, then straw.

Oh wow, our dens! The humans use excavators to dig holes sixty feet (18 meters) long and six feet (2 meters) deep. A concrete company donates long metal or concrete tubes that go from ground level all the way back to the actual dens, which are like small bedrooms. In the den, the temperature is always the same: 60°F

(15°C). We can sleep, relax, or hide in our dens whenever we want. They keep us cool in summer and warm in winter. The bears, lions, and wolves get dens too.

By the time you're ready to leave your safe cages, your underground dens will be ready and waiting.

CHAPTER 10

TiGER TALK

Another part of rehab is learning that humans are capable of respecting us. One way they do this is by trying to speak our language. As you get rehabilitated, you'll make all kinds of normal tiger noises, and the humans will usually understand what you're

This looks like a roar, but it's really a yawn.

communicating. Pat speaks our language fluently!

We rarely roar like lions, and we don't purr like housecats. But when we want to give a friendly greeting, we make a puffing sound called a chuff. It's like a soft *brrrr*. Moms might also chuff to comfort their cubs. In captivity, we may chuff at humans just to say hello, or let them know we're excited to see them. You may not know already, so here's how:

- Close your mouth.

- Blow through the nostrils and grunt a little at the same time.

- Listen to your breathy snort. *Chuffle, chuffle!*

Pat and Kent make friendly sounds with us too, though they sound more like a puff: *fff-fff-fff.*

SPEAKING TIGER

We communicate in other ways besides chuffing.

Head bumps: You know how dogs sniff one another's backsides when they meet for the first time or when they reunite? Our version of that is to gently bump heads. A head butt may be paired with a chuff. It's similar to a handshake, like we're saying, "Yay! Here we are together!"

Groan: A soft sound made with our mouths partially or fully closed. We make this sound while walking with our heads down.

Growl: We do this to tell others to go away!

Grunt: Same as growling, though we may also grunt when we want to mate.

Hiss: Just like housecats do! This lets others know we want them out of our space. We may also meow.

Moan: This is a soft, calm roar that can mean we're either content or uncomfortable. Tiger mothers often moan when they want their cubs to follow their directions or try new things.

Purr: We do this to show interest and draw others to us, especially for mating.

Roar: We do this rarely, but you can hear it from almost two miles (more than 3 kilometers) away. In the wild we'd have roared when taking down large prey or letting females know we want to mate. When we're nervous, our roar may sound like a cough.

Snarl: We do this when we feel we're in danger. A mother may snarl to keep other animals and even male tigers away from her offspring.

HUMAN WORDS

Of course, Pat and the others can't help using their human words with us. They usually say things like this:

 "Yes, you're a very big tiger."

 "You're a good tiger, Kamal. You're a good boy."

 "Oh, I know the sun feels so good on your fur. It feels so good for a cat. Yeah, I know . . . big purrs."

🐾 "Oh boy, that tall grass feels better than your old cage, doesn't it?"

Me and Diesel with Casey. Casey speaks tiger, too.

98

CHAPTER 11

GOOD TIMES

Mostly, rehab is about learning to enjoy being a tiger in your habitat. You'll see what I mean when you get to know your space. Let me describe a day in my life. You'll develop a routine, too. It'll probably be similar to mine, but each tiger lives in his or her own way.

Since it's winter now, I'll describe my favorite way to spend a summer day. Midafternoons are just too hot, so I crawl into my den for a delightful several-hour snooze. The cool concrete feels good against my warm fur.

When I lope out, I head slowly to the pond, which (if we've had a rainy spring) is full enough to submerge my huge body. If I'm

Time flies when you're having fun (and napping)!

lucky, the ducks and their ducklings are there. I'm still sleepy, but I wake up fast when my hunting instinct kicks in. Even though I'm not too hungry, I'll still stalk them quietly, expertly hiding in the tall reeds and cattails in my mini-ravine. There, I'm invisible.

I wade into the cool pond a bit, getting just the lower part of my legs wet. When the mama or papa duck notices me, they trick me every single time. He or she pretends to be injured and weak, so that I'll follow them and plan my attack. By then, their babies have moved far enough away from the parent. When I get close enough, mama or papa flies away toward the babies, who, thanks to their parent's trickery, have stayed safe from me.

Birds are clever. I never end up catching any ducks. Still, it's an adventure.

I usually stay for an hourlong relaxing soak in the shallow part of the pond. Soon enough, Simon will want to play. He'll wander in and lie down, getting as flat as possible so I see only his face and ears. I can never resist this invitation from Simon. I'll approach him and gently pounce (not the hunting kind!).

We start our wrestling match and move into deeper water, the best place to play my favorite game: Jump and Dunk. It's my favorite move—boinging up above Simon's big head, then dunking it underwater. But I hold it there for only a few seconds. I don't want to hurt the guy; I'm just having a little fun. Also, as much as we like water, we hate water in our eyes—so much that we'll even walk into the pond backward to avoid it.

Eventually we both head over to the shade of a cottonwood tree to dry off and relax, lying about twenty feet (6 meters) apart. The slight breeze on our damp fur feels great. We'll relax and fall asleep on our backs, exposing our white bellies to the strong, bright sunshine. Once we're completely dry, we may feel too hot again. Then we just repeat our whole routine! Sophie usually wants to splash around with us a little, though she doesn't wrestle.

Later, if it's our lucky day, someone will throw a Tiger Pie over the fence—or a whole raw chicken or even my favorite, a slab of raw steak!

Chase, who's slowly improving with his rehab, has been swimming a little, too. Mostly he's been enjoying sitting in the tall prairie grass in his habitat, and he's got something to say about that.

Ahhh.

Great Green Grass
An acrostic poem by Chase

Great for hiding.
Really tall.
A way to camouflage.
Safe and protected.
Someday soon, I may stop
    hiding all the time.

CHAPTER 12

PLAY TiME

Exercise and movement are important parts of our lives. So is play, even to us adults. You're not going to believe what our tiger playgrounds look like.

We start sanctuary life by playing in the just-for-tigers waterfall near the Round House. It's a big cement pool full of water, and cool water gushes down hard from a big plastic tube high above. It's awesome in the summer, but we love water all year long, more than any other species of cat (especially housecats!). We even love it frozen—we'll use our powerful paws to break through the ice. Remember, our ancestors were from Siberia.

And because we have webbed feet, we're powerful swimmers. In the wild, we can swim twenty miles (32 kilometers) without stopping! The waterfall is a great place to meet other tigers and learn to make friends,

POOL PARTY!

Me and Simon ... as good as life gets!

because it's "neutral territory"—it doesn't belong to any individual tiger, unlike each slice of the Round House. The humans notice which tigers play well together, and consider buddying them up forever in a habitat.

Simba's happy place.

I'm a water boy.

Nevada, Sierra, and Lilly playing Boomer Ball!

My huge concrete jungle.

I don't go to the waterfall anymore because I've been rehabbed for a long time and I have my pond. But when newly arrived tigers play in the waterfall, they feel like cubs again, even better. There are two gentle streams and a few small shady caves for hiding and relaxing.

And as I mentioned, each habitat has a play

PLAYGROUNDS

These giant spools once held long pieces of metal cable. Now they hold Natalya, Gary, and Alena!

Lions like spools, too. Here's Baby Leo, Agata, and Masai.

structure. Local businesses donate all kinds of materials—huge pieces of wood, ladders, barrels, thick rope, and lots more. Casey and Ryan love the challenge of figuring out ways to use the stuff they receive, and they sketch out all their wild and crazy ideas for playgrounds. Then they have a great time building them.

One of the most popular tiger play structures is a stack of several different tables, because we love to climb up high. Lions get giant wooden spools to roll around. Because leopards love stalking from up high, they get a "sky bridge." All of us big cats like ramps and high perches because we love to see everything in our territory.

Then there are toys. Boomer balls are specially designed for big cats and bears. They're my favorite. We can play really hard with them; they won't break. We can stretch on them, scratch them, pound them, swat them, and throw them. We used to play with bowling balls that a bowling alley donated, but the way we threw them around was just too dangerous!

PART 4

RELEASE

Making Up for Lost Time

CHAPTER 13

FiRSt FRESH STEPS

One day soon, the metal gate of your safe cage will open. Your favorite meat sits a few feet from the door. It's your release—your first taste of freedom.

You'll become stronger and steadier on your feet, just like me.

What Is Home?
by Chase

Home is tumbleweeds rolling by on the dirt road near my habitat.

Home is the crisp, cool air of the Rocky Mountains.

Home is hiding in the tall prairie grass for as long as I want.

Home is the top of my own wooden tower.

Home is the sound of the food truck coming with fresh meat when I least expect it.

Home is dust rising on the dirt roads as vehicles pass through.

Home is my perfect den.

With one brave, small step out of your safe cage, you're turning the first page in the book of your new story—the story of a good

A YEAR IN THE HIGH PLAINS OF COLORADO

After your first steps out of your safe cage, days will turn to weeks. Weeks turn to months. Months turn to years. You'll get into a rhythm and you'll learn how this place looks and feels in each season.

Chilly Chase!

WINTER: TIGERS OF THE TUNDRA

Lots of snow equals lots of white, powdery play. It's usually dry as a desert here, but winter and spring can be muddy. But it's almost always sunny and bright, so most of the staff don't mind being outside even on the coldest days (as in below zero).

life. The sadder pages of your story are behind you. You'll explore your huge new habitat in your own sweet time.

Me and Simon . . . we're made for this!

SPRING: WILDFLOWERS AND MELTING SNOW

Rivers start to flow hard as snow melts. The alpine pastures explode with wildflowers. In March, groggy bears shuffle out of their dens, their winter hibernation over.

Old Masai in the spring dusk.

Natasha, waking up after a long winter in her den.

SUMMER: WHEN IT'S HOT, IT'S HOT!

As in, over 100°F (38°C) hot. Then there are the crazy Colorado monsoons, when clouds suddenly appear from nowhere, and the sky roars, rumbles, and explodes with water. Then, as fast as the rain came, it stops, and sunlight dances around the canyons like it's showing off. The storms cool everything down, but the heat comes back fast! There's still snow on the Rockies, though, because they're so high.

On the hottest summer days, Sophie and I are so grateful for our pond.

FALL: WHEN ALL GOLD TURNS GREEN

All at once, aspen trees turn gold. Before long, it seems like the sky has dropped a bright red, orange, and yellow quilt over all of the Rockies. But soon enough, as winter comes, that blanket turns bright white again . . . for another winter.

Rainbows appear all year long . . . .

Most animals here love the rain. It really perks us up, and the humans say it's great to visit the sanctuary just after a good rainstorm. Clouds and storms can come in fast over the mountains, and they leave just as quickly. Often, the storms leave a rainbow behind, maybe as a goodbye gift for the human visitors who always get excited about the huge, multicolored band.

CHAPTER 14

MiLE INTθ THE WILD

Once you're fully released into permanent habitats, you may find that you're in view of lots of humans (not just staff and volunteers).

Staff and volunteers built this amazing walkway.

THE DiFFERENCE BETWEEN SANCTUARiES AND ZØOS

The people who run zoos may want to treat animals well, and they may teach people about animals, but most were built long ago when concrete and steel cages and pens were the usual habitats. Plus, most zoos are small because they're in cities, where there is not much open space.

Some zoos reduce the number of animals they have to give them more room, but most don't. Here though, we don't have much to do with people. We get lots of peace and quiet, and really, we do whatever we want. That's usually not true for zoo animals.

The Mile into the Wild is a long red iron walkway, like a skywalk, thirty feet (9 meters) above us, where human visitors (a hundred thousand every year!) can look down on us. Most of them have never been to an animal sanctuary, and at the end of their visit, they often say they could never go to a zoo again—and that they have never seen such calm animals.

We can be so relaxed because we hardly notice the humans on the walkway. We're protective of our land and water, but we don't think of the air and sky as our territory. So when people are walking above us, we're almost totally unaware of them. That's why visitors don't see us pacing around like animals in zoos. Zoo animals feel threatened with humans right in front of them. But here, if we seem freaked out by noise, we get to live farther away from the platform, where people can't see us.

I watched the humans build the whole platform a few years ago. They worked really hard, but I certainly didn't. They said I was quite a majestic construction-site supervisor!

I suppose the only thing that ever bothers me is when visitors on the Mile into the Wild don't give me my respect. This happens

Storms and sun over the mile.

rarely, and a volunteer guide just asks them to stop. The visitors might call out and tease me loudly, saying, for instance, "Here, kitty kitty kitty! Meow, meow!" Or they might get rowdy, stomping or running loudly on the walkway. They probably don't mean to bother us; they just don't know how smart we are. But somehow, we can sense that they're mocking us, and we hear the disrespect in their voices. Thankfully, this hardly ever happens.

WORDS ALONG THE MILE

People who donate money to the sanctuary get to pick quotes to put on plaques on the railings.

"Unless someone like you cares a whole awful lot, nothing is going to get better. It's not."
—DR. SEUSS, THE LORAX

"Forgive humanity for its ignorance, selfishness, and stupidity—here you are loved, safe, and adored . . . forever."
—ANONYMOUS

"Clearly, animals know more than we think and think a great deal more than we know."
—IRENE M. PEPPERBERG, PHD

"Our task must be to free ourselves by widening our circle of compassion to embrace all living creatures and the whole of nature and its beauty."
—ALBERT EINSTEIN

"Some people talk to animals. Not many listen though."
—A. A. MILNE

"Keep fighting for animal rights. You may lose your mind, but you'll find your soul."
—ANONYMOUS

123

CHAPTER 15

THE TIME OF YOUR LIFE

Eventually life starts to feel normal. You'll not only be content; you'll probably be delighted. For me and most healthy, happy tigers, it all boils down to two things: *getting* and *having*.

By "getting," I mean receiving and checking out new stuff. Any surprise the humans throw into my habitat—food, toys, other new things—is fascinating to me. I spend lots of time sniffing it and pawing at it.

By "having," I mean owning. It doesn't really matter what it is. If the humans throw in a bale of hay, my goal is simply to possess it. I guard it, making sure Simon and Sophie know it's mine, at least for a while (though once I've had enough, I'll share). If I get a whole turkey, it feels like a Christmas present. I hold it between my huge paws and nuzzle it for a while, just enjoying the experience of having it before I eat it.

You'll start to learn all the things that delight you, too. You'll get plenty and you'll have plenty.

Now go run, roar, and roll.

Swim, stretch, and snooze in your den.

Chuff, puff, and sniff.

Scratch where it itches, soak in your cool pond, and splash in the soothing whoosh of the waterfall.

Gorge, growl, and get wet.

Cheers!

Do head butts, do chin bumps, and nuzzle your muzzle against a log.

Stand tall and proud. Feel free and whole.

Because here you are: thirty-nine lucky tigers. Ready for the time of your life!

A LETTER FROM THE AUTHOR:
BEING THEIR VOICE

When we welcome new human life into the world, we welcome our babies into the company of other creatures. We paint animals on the walls. We don't paint cell phones. We don't paint work cubicles. We paint animals to show them that we are not alone. We have company. And every one of those animals in every painting of Noah's ark, deemed worthy of salvation, is in mortal danger now, and their flood is us.

—Carl Safina, TED TALK,
What Are Animals Thinking and Feeling?

There were only two reasons I wanted to write this book—because I could, and because I'm a human.

The gift of being alive is meant for all creatures. But humans have another gift: being able to use words to make a point, to speak out against unfairness. Often, our words can help change the world and make it better.

But nonhuman animals can't speak up for themselves. Tigers and other endangered animals will never be able to educate humans about how their habitats are shrinking, how they're being killed for fun and money, how they're being used for entertainment, how they're being bought and sold as pets. They won't explain to the world what's happening to them and their species, or describe their suffering. They can't stick up for themselves and present their argument to humans who might be able to help. They will just quietly disappear. They'll fade away and never walk on Earth again.

Only two things—words and photos—make up this book. But I hope that what's printed on these pages can help tigers and all other creatures in trouble. Because the more you know, the more you can do to help.

— Kama Ainhon

I'm inside one of the (empty!) rescue cages that get loaded into trucks. I'm thinking about what the animals who've spent time in it might say if they could talk.

ONE BIG QUESTION FOR PAT CRAIG

Q. How do you deal with all the sad stories?

A. Within my own world I have to find a way to greet each day with renewed hope and enthusiasm—and I do so with a full belief that other humans can do the same.

That way, I never carry any bad feelings forward and don't expect others to either. It helps to believe that everyone on this planet has at least some good in their heart, and those who act unkindly or irresponsibly have only temporarily forgotten how to use their minds to make things better.

In thirty-seven years of operating a sanctuary, I can tell you there have been a thousand times in my life where the world outside has turned pitch black! There have been countless nights when I had a deep feeling of failure, and sometimes I feel an overwhelming sense that our work is just not seen by the outside world.

Yet no matter how bad I feel, with each beat of my heart I'm reminded that life goes on and that I need to remain strong. So many lives depend on my ability to truly believe.

As long as someone is willing to respond to the need for help, there is always an option on the table.

Running a true sanctuary for animals takes incredible focus and dedication. The path we are on is so extremely narrow and dangerous that it's never okay to lose your own desire to live, work, and make the animals your top priority.

For without our empathy and compassion, they have nothing. And so we go on.

Believe in yourself, and believe in other humans, no matter how sad the animals' stories. Each morning brings a new beginning and the opportunity for each of us to look in the mirror with hope and confidence.

HOW YOU CAN HELP
TIGERS AND OTHER WILDLIFE

🐾 **Tell** others what you've learned in this book. Keep learning, and continue to be a teacher by letting people know that though wild animals may be adorable, beautiful, or fascinating, they aren't pets or playthings.

🐾 **Visit** WildAnimalSanctuary.org to learn even more about the sanctuary. You can even "adopt" Kamal or any other animal there and get yearly photos with updates on how they're doing.

🐾 **Donate** money to the sanctuary, or to any animal sanctuary near you. You might collect change in a jar (the pennies are the same copper color as Simon the tiger!). It costs $8,000 each year to take care of just one tiger, lion, or bear, and it costs $19 million a year to run WAS.

🐾 **Write** to your local zoo and tell them your opinion about animals in captivity. Ask them not to breed tigers (or any animal) unless the breeding is an official part of the Species Survival Plan, which helps endangered animals.

🐾 **Remember**—if your family has a cat, or is thinking about adopting one, tell your parents about the problems tigers have when they're declawed, and ask them not to do this to your kitty if scratching the furniture is a problem. There are other, better solutions; talk to your vet about them.

🐾 **Travel** humanely. If your family takes a trip and wants to see local wildlife, carefully research the sanctuaries you are considering visiting. It's safe to assume that any sanctuary that asks tourists for money to let them hold the animals is not treating those animals well. For instance, leashed monkeys that will perch on your shoulder do not have happy, normal lives.

 Avoid zoos, even if you want to see and learn about wild animals up close. You can learn by watching videos online. If you do go, look closely and notice how the animals are treated. How big are their cages? Do they seem bored or anxious? Are they fed a diet that is close to their natural diet? If you can, ask the keepers or other zoo staff your questions.

 Avoid circuses or shows in which wild animals are used for entertainment.

There are lots more ways to lend tigers a helping hand.

GLOSSARY

breed: to produce babies

captivity: kept by humans (as in zoos or as pets); the opposite of living in the wild

carnivore: an animal that eats meat

empathy: caring about and being able to imagine how another person or animal is feeling

endangered: close to becoming extinct

exotic: foreign and unusual

extinct: no longer existing

habitat: the natural home of an animal

hormones: special chemicals animals' bodies make to help them do certain things

majestic: like royalty

malnourished: not fed a proper diet

neuter: to perform an operation that keeps male animals from getting females pregnant

recover: to get better

refuge: a safe place

rehabilitate: to return to one's natural state of physical and emotional health

release: to let go

rescue: to save or help

territory: the land or space an animal lives in

transport: to move from one place to another

vulnerable: easily hurt

BiBLi0gRAPHY

Jazynka, Kitson. *Mission: Tiger Rescue: All About Tigers and How to Save Them.* Washington, DC: National Geographic Kids, 2015.

Marsh, Laura. *National Geographic Readers: Tigers.* Washington, DC: National Geographic, 2012.

Simon, Seymour. *Big Cats.* New York: HarperCollins, 1991.

Walker, Sarah. *Eyewonder: Big Cats: Open Your Eyes to a World of Discovery.* New York: DK Children's, 2014.

PHOTO CREDITS

Bengal by Corbis/SuperStock: 56

Cheetah by Digital Vision/Getty Images:54

Indochinese Tiger by Anankkml/Dreamstime: 56

Snow Leopard by PhotoLink/Photodisc/Getty Images: 55

Siberian Tiger by Andy Gehrig/iStockphoto.com/Getty Images: 56

South China Tiger by abcphotosystem/Shutterstock: 56

Sumatran Tiger by Karina Walton/Alamy: 56

ACKNOWLEDGMENTS

Big chuffs of appreciation to:

Pat Craig

Kent Drotar

Becca Miceli

Casey Craig

Ryan Clements

Sam Sherrow and Athena Rose Wang

Jamey Hecht

Erica Zappy Wainer

And all the staff and volunteers of the
Wild Animal Sanctuary

INDEX

Note: Page references in italics indicate photographs.

▫ TRUE TALES ᴏꜰ RESCUE ▫

Kama Einhorn is a humane educator, animal welfare advocate, and author of more than forty books for children and teachers. Animals are her people. She lives in Brooklyn, New York.